I want to be a Scientist

Other titles in this series:

I WANT TO BE A
Scientist

DAN LIEBMAN

FIREFLY BOOKS

A FIREFLY BOOK

Published by Firefly Books Ltd. 2016

First Printing

Publisher Cataloging-in-Publication Data (U.S.)

Names: Liebman, Daniel, author.
Title: I want to be a scientist / Dan Liebman.
Description: Richmond Hill, Ontario, Canada : Firefly Books, 2016. | Series: I want to be a— | Summary: "A picture book for children who want to know how to become a scientist, what a scientist does, and what makes it fun" — Provided by publisher.
Identifiers: ISBN 978-1-77085-790-2 (hardcover) | 978-1-77085-789-6 (paperback)
Subjects: LCSH: Scientists — Juvenile literature. | Science – Vocational guidance – Juvenile literature.
Classification: LCC Q147.L543 |DDC 502.3 – dc23

Library and Archives Canada Cataloguing in Publication

Liebman, Daniel, author
        I want to be a scientist / Dan Liebman.

(I want to be a)
ISBN 978-1-77085-789-6 (paperback).--ISBN 978-1-77085-790-2 (hardback)

        1. Science--Vocational guidance—Juvenile literature.
2. Scientists—Juvenile literature. I. Title.

Q147.L54 2016   j502.3   C2016-901039-2

Published in the United States by
Firefly Books (U.S.) Inc.
P.O. Box 1338, Ellicott Station
Buffalo, New York 14205

Published in Canada by
Firefly Books Ltd.
50 Staples Avenue, Unit 1
Richmond Hill, Ontario L4B 0A7

Photo Credits:

© Parisa Michailidis: page 5
© Photodiem/shutterstock.com: pages 6–7
© Abd. Halim Hadi/Shutterstock.com: page 8
© Phil Degginger/Alamy Stock Photo: page 9
© Andor Bujdoso/shutterstock.com: page 10
© Dragon Images/shutterstock.com: page 11
© Microgen/Shutterstock.com: page 12
© Allexxandar/Shutterstock.com: page 13

© Grant Heilman Photography: pages 14
© Grant Heilman Photography: pages 15
© St. Michael's College School: page 16
© science photo/Shutterstock.com: page 17
© Andrey Armyagov/Shutterstock.com: page 18–19
© Alexander Raths/Shutterstock.com: page 20
© michaeljung/Shutterstock.com: page 22, 23
© A and N photography/Shutterstock.com: page 21

The Publisher acknowledges the financial support for our publishing program by the Government of Canada through the Canada Book Fund as administered by the Department of Canadian Heritage.

Printed in China

What is a scientist? What does a scientist do?

Scientists are people who solve problems. They like to know how things work.

There are different kinds of scientists. Scientists who study plants and animals are called "biologists."

Marine biologists are scientists who study plants and animals that live in the water.

Scientists who study fossils of plants and animals are called "paleontologists."

Computer scientists program and design computers.

Scientists find answers to questions such as "What does something look like when it is many times bigger?"

Archaeologists study the past. They dig for coins, tools and other things left by people who lived a long time ago.

Where do stars come from? Scientists who study the sky and the planets are called "astronomers."

Geologists study rocks in order to learn about the history of the Earth.

Botanists study plants and flowers.

These students are looking at a lizard called a "bearded dragon." Scientists who study animals are called "zoologists."

Scientists also make robots. This scientist is studying robotics.

It takes a rocket scientist to send an astronaut into space.

Some astronauts are scientists, too.

This is a model of something that is too small to see without a microscope. Scientists use models to help them study objects.

Scientists must stay safe because sometimes their work is dangerous. This scientist is wearing goggles and gloves.

Scientists always want to learn more. They sometimes start out as assistants.

Being a scientist is an important job. Scientists are like detectives. They look for answers to problems.

What kind of scientist would you like to be? Here is a list of what some scientists do:

An anthropologist studies human beings

An archaeologist studies life from long ago

An astronomer studies the sky and planets

A biologist studies living things

A botanist studies plants and flowers

A chemist studies chemical elements, such as oxygen

A computer scientist studies computers

An entomologist studies insects

A geologist studies rocks

A marine biologist studies living things in the ocean and other bodies of water

A meteorologist studies the weather

A paleontologist studies prehistoric life and fossils – including dinosaurs

A seismologist studies earthquakes

A volcanologist studies volcanoes

A zoologist studies animals